HOPE
and
SUBSTANCE

Dianne Cikusa

Copyright © 2015 Dianne Cikusa

The moral right of the author has been asserted.

All rights reserved. No part of this book may be reproduced or transmitted by any person or entity, in any form or by any means, electrical or mechanical, including photocopying, recording, scanning or by any information storage and retrieval system, without prior permission in writing from the author and publisher.

Cataloguing-in-Publication entry is available from the National Library of Australia: http://catalogue.nla.gov.au

Author: Cikusa, Dianne, 1973–

Title: Hope and Substance

ISBNs: 978-0-9943257-4-7 (Paperback – colour images)
        978-0-9943257-5-4 (Paperback – black and white images)
        978-0-9943257-2-3 (epub)
        978-0-9943257-3-0 (mobi)

Subjects: Poetry

Photographer: Cikusa, Dianne, 1973–

Cover images: © Dianne Cikusa

Published by Mignon Press, 2015
PO Box 922, Katoomba NSW 2780

For Scott & Andy

Dead egg, I lie
Whole
On a whole world I cannot touch

Sylvia Plath, Ariel

Contents

Part 1: The Urban Forest 15

    Zebra Crossing 19

    Disintegration 22

    Looking-Glass 25

    Caracol (Snail) 28

    Waiting Room 31

Part 2: White Noise 35

    Turning Air into Water 39

    Ink Spots 53

    The Blue House 57

    Clearance Height 60

    Dressing the Skeleton 70

Part 3: The Reconstitution of Desire 75

    Milk and Honey 79

    Eclipse 95

    Parting Wave 98

    Private Address 102

Part 1: The Urban Forest

Zebra Crossing

*[mother won't let us
out of her emotional
asylum:]*

*three bags full sir;
creativity got stuffed in her
hand bag,
wonder bra got shrunk
during spin cycle;
embossed labelling: where is
the self-help manual for
terror?*

[double-breasted consumers]

*her brow is creasing
with facial lines
she sent the pet to
the drycleaners
(forgetting it was only
wednesday:)*

*thereafter, she was always
four days short
of an honest explanation
she looked smart in stripes
and so left us all
misbegotten,
leaning over into cracked earth*

*she smiles that
we are perplexed,
having stretched the boundaries
of friendship
and non-sexual favours*

**

no parachute of warning:
a freefall into hypocrisy

real black does not
argue with real white
he just announces:
your move, and she politely
advances

[to be enveloped by his
discreet arms]

**

under durable rooftops
are installed
a lonely blackboard
and a white typist—

my dearest sir, she writes,
if you keep interrupting me,
i will never be finished;

his studded apprehension
is obscured by the
glitter of her refracted
glances,
perfectiveness begins its steep
rise to the peak of
knowingness

slippery border will knock
loose her senses
(for better or worse)

he stepped away from
the kerb when she

*started sprouting obscenities
garden gnome was watching
the whole time,
crimson paint
dribbling down his chin
and staining his red boots*

*[cropped judgements
and littered snapshots]*

**

*element of fire
is
beginning to steal around
the edges of perceptivity;
we fall into deep love
then change our
bloodied mind
high incidences of revenge
aim to strike down
ardent leisures for
a share of enthusiasm*

*glimpsing down wishing wells:
it's a 40 foot drop
then we climb out wet,
spectacles taped to the
sides of our heads*

*bone-coloured bridesmaids
stay neutral to happiness*

[twenty-four hours]

*the danger of optimism—
is that of never coming down.*

Disintegration

[1]   an informal conservationist
       has restively sat,
       having barely taken a stand

       she wishes for moments
       of extra peace, or a
       moment of extraordinary peace;
       narratives are disposable—
       her vague tears already
       glossing over a new sequence

       hauled by vox populi, she is
       sapped and disgruntled
       by incomplete directions

≈ Following their degraded maps,
       she will scratch 'n' sniff
       the warpaint clean by noon

       ...
       ...

[2]   whilst disenchanted wives
       are disobeying house rules,
       husbands are measuring
       centimetres of pictorial conquest;
        insulated offspring
       claiming easy handholds,
       eroding mischief
       and according sizeable injuries

       desolation is applauded;
        trust a standing of thoroughbreds
         not to lose grip
        in the
       slush of caution

        Underfoot,
        sustenance has been slayed
         by frosted eyes
         and starched compulsions,
        those non-deserving heirs
         lacking time to
        scour the dirt which had
         rudely entered their
          mouths
         via greedy fingernails
        and contemptuous attitudes

          ...
        ...

[3]   turning pages: she is perusing
           the louvred topsoil of cityscapes
           nomads
           nursing muted heartbeat

           next door, fusty urbanites
           would fade in colourwash
           and a tea-party is hiding
           stowaways
           and sponsored beggars

       disarmament
           of technology had drawbacks:
           she was aghast to find
           illegible handwriting
           in superscript, and the
           televised version could not
           be dissected for bottlenecks

           bygones were gift-wrapped
           in sheets of
           influential love-letters
           torn from desiccated notepads

the orientation of man was stymied;
endangered bodyguards
and manic captors
needing also to be embosomed

wretched odyssey
is
lost in endless caverns of desire,
mature farmers starved of benefit
 and left unwatered
    [unwashed], rooted in
stooped sunshine at dusk, and
scorched projection on awakening

businessmen sleeping...
and toastmasters
left reeling in slumbering debate.

Looking-Glass

Trace your roots back to
skinned knees
and juvenile playgrounds...

We are schooled in self-praise
and visual ceremony,
  Smoking dispassionately
    as
the bleating infancy
of years ambles past,
blistering resentfully
as passing minutes have
learned artfully to despise

Callous ingratitude rouses us,
but we are never alarmed;
[imperviously] we brush off
the wallpaper and chalk dust—
pushovers from the monarch

      Telephone only /
listens to the
 fatiguing demeanors
of the cretin and the sweet-talker

Benevolence is underpinned by
the vestige of ugly name-tapes;
    reproachful rivals
& swank champions
imprinting with sniggers

Bigots with speckled origins
and migrating hatred
tripping up alphabetical roll-call

the dispirited milieu

obtains a brusque warrant,
only to incur
the next band of teams
enervating creed
and courting folly

Proud customs holding races
under tether   (though
 xenophobia
     is widening:)

Undaunted teabags steeped
in hostility; Perdition
creeping out per capita
sun-drenched descendants
with spotless teeth
and perforated waistlines
weeping
from saline gash;
raped coastlines
flanked by gullible outpost

Surging presumptions
and
insolent stares:
The beleaguered maestro
ingesting stanzas of acute
disagreement,
his cavities eating
mouthfuls of an insoluble topic

lyrical handshakes
and
pert confession
conjoined in a new class of deceit

are we coming? or going?

[: if and when] arrived
together

Though godhead does
not like preaching,
altruism is
openly pushing discourse
into freckled faces

Portable sunlight
would flourish by yanking
fraternal twins
of greed and evil: Amongst
brother and minikin,
selective pity
finds explosive energy in
in
egg cracks

For sisterhood,
singing anthem
rejoices in coloured feather.

Caracol (Snail)

menacing Persons, left behind
the shadow
of their passive insensitivity

[crushed housing]

Regards, city-siders
we accept
your delirious ovation,
and neatly recite
    leather-bound policy
on behalf of
those greased morsels
who never owned a voice
to publicise the anguish
of patented choice; glazed
will and self-raising skin

domestic squeals
permeated by human erotica

[de-beaked] performance
making quiet outcry—
splitting hairs
in barbed cages,
but ne'er on heartless heads

God gave them half
a chance to speak,
until world
made them swallow
such lethal doses
of cosmetic flaws;
 spirits,
drowning in accessories

lined stomachs
are spilling dignity;

I know you're green:
    it's those
vegetables
went down the wrong way,
carnivorous lust in reflux

...I'm rambling
    to protect my swollen testament

    gather my thoughts,
before you squash them carelessly

So haven't we all
recoiled
from the overt stench
of superior dialogue, cut and
pasted in social gridlock

Though we meant not
to gauge a relished reaction,
merely to mirror
the deafening mannerisms
that were hushing up pink faces

[Too late] now that
rigor mortis
got us
tongue-tied
under the table, blissfully
  Drinking a toast
  to
pretty conversational pieces
that would never
disturb the ecology,
(assuming we all politely agreed)

Here's a good pinch
    of snickering laxatives, yet
    to be administered by watering-can

    lucky lady sat on a
    cat with sixty-nine lives

    The humble bee,
     he sits on his own sting
    steaming weapons too easily
    evaporating his focus

    And didn't you know—
    by avoiding death,
        you were killing people.

(First appeared in *Cordite Poetry Review*, Issue #26)

Waiting Room

10.29 am.

The vocalist is cramped in
an auditorium, chained
to wordsmiths
of coarse palette and
fruitless zeal,
her cohorts sulking
on beer-sodden backseats

marooned
leopards recede into backdrops,
Love-birds
sighted on windowsills,
draining water-levels sip by sip

A pallid deer is marred
by tainted aspirations,
 bereft,
recalling the overhaul
of ornament and cardinal sin

lately
there isn't time for small talk
Since the drummer departed,
anarchy is
grating on syntax
and purple prose,
leaving the songstress in tears
and her audience displeased

1.51 pm.

Life in zigzag
finds the contentious captain
punctured and glorified,

spent on eyesores
and chomping after calories;
A lapse in deliberation
has the crew nonplussed,
mincing in
rudiments and lawless logic

colouring books are dirty
with dramatics
of frangipani and lei,
flamboyant teens rigged up
for grungy interaction
raked in adulterous approval
and belated morning glory;
Smiling anniversary
is appealing
to the daydreaming cadet
trussed up in euphoric spiel

Lifeline versus helplines:
only a
twenty-something is saved
from dyslexic prodding

raunchiness of
the rope-walker is untrained
against
slipping provocation
and maudlin occurrence;
His clarity is footworn,
whilst
diva is melodiously
skimming over
tandem programmes
and tariff, scrolling down
turquoise ambitions and
wafting priority, despite a
refrain of quickening pulse

5.22 pm.

The shockproof salesman is
struck by early lightning;
rangers caught him
cramming cherubs into
dollhouses and
sticking labels to stained glass,
his fortune mistimed this livid day

Quaking temptress left an
irate thunderbolt
eschewing
inside coffee bean templates
and toffee-nosed receipt,
Yet limply they sat: nobody
got up from their cushion
with credits rolling by the dozen

Split-seconds later—
would see them all
gushingly buried under rubble.

Part 2: White Noise

Turning Air into Water

i).

*virtual resources
are stretched,
and the captive fish
must accept his small square
of consciousness*

*his clear eyes surmise
from the other side of
the glass wall, thinking
how the world
is tanked
up on medication*

*he perceives on an
acquiescent wavelength,
as one does befriend the transition
of water
  //> martial art
  is cutting into conversation*

*(a close up:) on mossy fabric,
the plant life is entertaining
autonomy,
fascinating by acrobatics,
beastly admirers
taking care with time-lapsed
compliments*

*[they should
remove only decaying matter]*

ii).

mother is eating her
children again—consuming
them with her big eyes;
she's cursed with
umbilical fatigue (let go, ma,
it's off-season)
we are not affixed
to obligation;
children do not like to
be psychoanalysed without
their consent

malady is
bathed in early-morning siesta
 [bottled snores:]
wait 'til we show
absolute tendencies
before you harshly wake us up;
flabbergasted thud
of reality   > (are we
inside tinted-glass?)
the grass is an
altered shade of green

[she'll put us under
stricter supervision...]

jus--t
in
c—ase

()**&%#$!

His & Hers:
their classic outlines
will go astray from
a principal error--//
// he will blame her
for imperfect rule,

she will blame him
for inadequate safety

insurgent adrenalin
enlarges the corpuscles
of their contradiction,
professing that x
is greater than y—
then incumbent law
imparts a new consonant

iii).

: unverified
: uncertified
how long is a piece of string?
let's see ----- i'll estimate
99 metres with punctuation

substantively,
  we delete old generations
and kiss hectares goodnight

so little free room
outside the
diorama of communal fashion;
we are so
engrossed in groundwork,
we forget our hope revives in
brighter vicinity,
in the midst of
light-hearted companions
not under frantic attack
of forced guarantees
and
hungry compliance
they each can scarcely deliver

*astral lovers
feeding us fluid, so as
to hold us afloat like a buoy;
breath is
nibbling on our ear,
destiny is eternally gnawing on
raw cynicism
&
infinite humour
[would anyone fancy to bring
in the plain-clothes visitor??]*

*i remark that
 we will be highlighting
decorum
  and
sacrament*

iv).

*))   plunging irremissibly into
bricks and mortar occupation;
even the taxpayers are
getting tired by this
relentless
accrual
of the clock*

*standing egos wait
querulously,
exasperated stock prices
drop significantly
before the muted hours of our death;
the visionary is in a time warp
to which
rational flesh
will not surrender:
stop paying their way to*

*heaven—
even the gatekeeper has
overheads to account for;
we're all owing a tribute,
& you have to compensate
for where you went out of
control
  - - (- - Beliefs are rebounding) - -)*

*familiarity is cold
jellied meat no longer
satisfies the palate*

*[...at least, that's what
the soldier crab told me]*

v).

*an interjection
here:)*

*terrestrial lady—beneath
our decadent feet
is addressing her listeners:
in order of foreign language,
we will shrug off the
negative translation*

*<< you're regressing, and i'm
losing my mind trying to
convert flags
into tangible portions...*

*(occult has inhaled demons
the wrong way,
due to
the restlessness of stimuli)*

-----------> *grab the ripcord*
   and we'll
 land
you
on
linoleum,
 bitumen faces
may begin to stare at
you inquisitively
from every corner of the
hospital globe;
where you could not contain
your toxic thoughts
they became a street hazard,
upon which spectators
could administer advice
regarding indefensible neglect

[repulsive hatred
is self-hatred in replay:]

vi).

crossed
my
heart

and hoped
to
die
    X
     X
   X

   X
  X
   X

vii).

*hysterical scars of
an inflamed woman, annunciating
from pluto's outskirts;
  screams dilated
her pupils circulate
the diameter of unborn fright*

*(soundtracks
infusing in double-room)*

*when her blood is ripe,
the poet will cup
her breasts
words will fill images
and her agony
will stop sobbing—
he will understand that
she
is making ode to the darkness*

*hallowed man knows
when candles
are burning low, exacting a
luxuriant puff of comprehension;
his smoking hands
resolve to
embrace her dutifully*

*it is no wonder
he cannot hold a single tear—
she is leaking profusely
sadness hopes to be captured,
but the heart
does not like to be
squeezed
and so he is hurting
her again*

(options are diminishing   ):

*must she die with
bruises, reminiscent of his
compulsive emigration?
there are no stoplights
in this disconsolate country*

*so then glamour retreats—
she is by chance crudely
safer in caves of indistinction,
 though
somewhat colourless //:   //:*

 *[counterpoised], she needs
her mind to sit comfortably
beside her
whilst volume is racing*

*intrinsically,
heaven is slowing down
to allow her to jump
on to the next airbus;   a briefing:
when embarking on cosmic planes,
ticket stubs
get issued at the conductor's whim*

hit-or-miss—

*(+ but +) don't mix'n'match
      the
         passengers
            in
           open range /*

_ _ * _ _

_ _ * _ _

\- \- * \- \-

\- \- * \- \-

(an) impetus:

spinning
 on the rim of garnered
 assumption,
his challenge is to
remain a catalyst, in spite of
an urge to conquer
(his vigour will
be swiftly devoured)

he hesitates
the grid is slipping—but is also
choosing moments that
will later
disperse down spiral stairs

 liquify,
 simplify

take her in highest arms

\#\#

 erase the complex,
 &
the complicated...

... ever so gently, jot down
 linguistic history
 &
fictive deficiency

like a fickle ornament,

*she's always
on the verge of
        falling,*

   breaking

 *band-aid
needing salvage, rescue*

\# \#

*belittled princess
and her pea*

*enlivened,
  then censured*

□ □

*adventitiously, we could integrate
a cartoon hero 'bout now
 (: someone like that convivial guy
 from the fluorescent series:)
we will enjoy animated rendition,
and he will replenish description
by way of his jovial transmitter*

(carefree ♠)

*repair us
  to the present-day*

viii).

*insured for a medium
shelf-life: the doll is
well-preserved
in plastic, her sweet cheeks*

*pulsing under humid gaze;
she makes enticing gestures
to those who can't
afford a knockback
from her lipstick display*

*(can you distinguish five persons,
    all singled out,
at the point-of-purchase)   ?*

i can

*basket
case
trolley*

*take your wicked choice,
or make a reputable pick   ¿¿¿*

ix).

*whoops! the milky way
 has smeared
in hypochondria*

*celestial weights are
heaving down
 internal life is suffocating,
restitution
is of pitiable form
  when genes are flipped
out of control*

*(bend and stretch)
once,
  twice,
    three times*

press record

*& repeat again these
rustic fundamentals*

x).

yours truly,

*introducing psychics
&
pseudonyms—
the skies' preview declares an
oceanfront of roiling vantage;
spirits tripping over themselves
in procrastination,
d i t h e r i n g,
 dallying
in the tropic of cancer*

*refer your tender complaints
to the doctor;
wax museum is listening only
to the camouflaged moods of
incandescent statues,
escapism
is fast running its
fingers through stranded hair*

*[invisible teapots
marshalling lost tour guides]*

imperceptibly))))))))

*and perhaps
they could have catered
a little more
generously to light eaters;*

*the opera singer
would have neither lost her voice
from biting so many pursed lips
nor from dipping six-packs of cookies
into virulent natures*

*jobs would have been
well done
and condiments finished /-/
 but instead,
they snack on simmering insults
and cumbersome conceit*

*why
is there
no sorbet on the menu?
we are certain
that we pre-booked dessert*

*(recant the burnt toast
of repetition):
we've spruced up
the same campaign, albeit
its recognition took on
an extra-special character*

[i hear an executive chuckle]

hi there,

*guess
who promoted
dinner
as 'being' the show?*

*fat-cheeked man is
losing his teeth by the dozen
santa stopped bringing real
presents long ago*

*(...most probably on account of
all the ingurgitated gratitude   )))*

*glacé harmony sneaks
a divine peek
inside the other sandwich,
 silently
drooling saliva,
in the hope that
its beneficiaries will die of
 an intervention—
thus forfeiting the whippings
 of
their privileges,*

*and nullifying
  the
presence of any doubt.*

Ink Spots

i)

The amoebas are running
in circles:
 amphetamine clock

They ask
that you do your best service
before the funeral,
since jollity knows when
the mob shall disband
from a posterior standpoint

*...while you were busy
    gazing at starlets...*

Misery,
  is investing all one's
worth in a singular moment,

&/
 or
  numbly
   fooling
    around
     on the
    fringes
of integrity

ii)

Turning up nostrils
at gruelling local breezes,
we suffered the strains
of grain-fed brutality

and loosened fruit;
pod-like
 remnants of a butchered hearth
and bleeding yokes

(:)) His livid eye,
 is leaking reckless tyranny

 we will grimly submit;
 summation of boy-girl-boy

 ∧

 alerting—

 Look once more, for what
 we have missed

iii)

Time in rewind:
 try plotting points
The compass
draws between mother and son
and their supple meanderings
 (: yet East
does not easily pervade West ((

Connecting
  threads
implies
  darning
the
  dress
of
  an
amended
  tradition,

with
intimate meanings
& codes encrypted:)

   Tick
     tock

time and again, we run from death,
probing under pantaloons
to find favour
of our affluence,
 like moneyed fellows
sold into paradise—
whose primeval delight
rejuvenates in hypothetical wombs

 NB: Refurbishments to continue
 after every mercantile downpour

      [: Inserting a
          paltry discount
        for parasols
     laced with
   steely vexation]

The invincible producer
directing
poisonous commercials; > > > implanting
an intrusion of fanfare—
hors d'oeuvres and sea-horses
The ploys
of psychological games

iv)

Stills: female shows signs
of madness
as they expand

her corsets beyond horizons—###
Incomprehensible tortures

[she gave a
        yielding
  exhibition]

The next lift takes us to
west wing,
where we are visited
by
Storyboard children,
flipping through candy menus
And sharing
output from lolly dispensary:/
/// sugary bombs
and crackling taste buds

bumping into lamp posts
en route to corner stores

meanwhile—

luminous Faery weaves his
summers' mosaic and winter
tapestry
To hang in forest walls,

[dropping petty stitches
    onto sticky leaves]

when questioned,
  he retracts inside the mantle
of season,

Where bleached sky
would too soon prise wisdom
from his gracious struggle.

The Blue House

Her understudy
    is
      sleepwalking
  above the ceiling ...
      ...
    ...
...
...
 ... fresh paint
     is
       shaking
   them
both
  free
    of
 their
...   ...   reverie ...   ...
     ...   ...
       ...
          ...

Syllables are crying
for inspiration—
     ): a sedate phrase)
drops a radiant hint
on her theatrical canvas
(laid in meshing pixels)

broken skulls and
chipped insights,
    deadlines unmet
Brilliance is bountiful
when ovaries
are bursting with memory

[we pass through to a
palliative sanctuary:]

one-eyed vision
 is puréed in ritual disdain
and habitual scoff

toiling among yearnings,
we find
crayons lodged in embryo

The moored changeling
avers a cruel deviation;
her volatility was
residing upstairs,
waiting
for unfolding fingers
to grasp discovery
 Unborn foetus
touching his own curled toes

[she's scared to be a ghost]

pastel wanderers appear sinister
when confronted by
giant light-bulbs

silhouettes become frightening
when they
are reflecting no sound

belligerence
is transmitting voices,
and fear is duplicating them

she is stifled by tight
intimations, conduct
escaping under lucid skin,
pastoral promises
impregnated
with perinatal outfit
the child is sun-dried

Devil's lesson will ask her:
"What shapes grandeur?"

(feigned intuition
    replacing ostentation)

From the motherland,
we spot
sublime mediators
stroking fervour,
and environmental actors
exchanging episode
between
their quibbling selves

They love the surface of
drama
and she, plagued by guilt,
is too willing to
smear over their hidden debt
with reddened profanities

an easel
is her instrument of joy

... stabbing paintbrush

akin to an umbrella
poking quietly in the back.

Dedicated to the Mexican painter Frida Kahlo de Rivera
(1907-1954)

Clearance Height

I.

Outside the domain of
conventional freedom,
we
construct
an unseen podium

conceptual cameras eyeing
the inflections of mind

[same location]
[new situation]

           : in sync
and scru-
     tin-
   ising

here's the latest:

II.

Evening news-hound
is hyped to place an arbitrary
order for leavened bread;
  breaking new crust
he will report
undertakings from
roadworthy positioning

[expatiate]
[emaciate]

give > over to the infernal

[solidified] Charades
of man and species—
man _is_ specimen to the
siren of venerable kind,
  (should he
awaken a special interest)

presently, her watchman
is surveying them
through arching eyebrows

∷ ∷ ∷ (she is building indications)

This belle

  is

extra
ordinary

III.

Take a seat: The sea-level
is objective
where one's ego
has been watered down

how so? we've not an inkling
...?
  ...?
    ...?

ask Geronimo:
he did spot
  veracity from above,
     ...
       ...
         ...

...
...
...
during
an
immense leap of faith
...
...
...
...
...
...

nor
did anybody mention
The Golden Flight:
allusions to
the ethereal,
excursions to
 ephemeral
and unaffected places...

{ open sesame }
Find the key to
access all areas

left then right

in here, it's roomy & resilient
come and be validated,
even the discards
are snapped up

out there,
lavish consumption
comes at an additional
(and rather unflattering) cost

Or,

just linger if you will

now choose a), b), or c)

leave nobody dangling—
in case you brazenly dash off

or randomly splash out
on

the lovely,
   the marvelous,

      and the idyllic;

IV.

i
  o
    u

[How much

          ]?

This much
and more]

Stealthily,
parent companies
were preening their figures
into grandiose
proportion; Outdated assurance
and obsolete changes,
    sluggish dynamics
Results are now outsourced;

produced work
is submerged back into production

Waves of migrants,
leaving behind lost causes
 well, why not?
greet the roman numeral

ex-partner will find you
in the dark
(and esteem
 is easily thrown overboard)
 ? ? did they imagine you'd
 be okay?

wait to dial ooo

Plankton affirms that
the mercurial fishing line has
caught
on every creative throat

V.

Energy matters—thus
a fertile awareness
is built up by a
commodious approach

Your anatomy finds
its filter in graced physique;
      discernment
opens up the fault lines
of childhood, revealing
 subconscious betrayal—
you were perpetrating from
the inside;

The educated guile of a
hollow psyche
has unwarily hit upon asphalt

In box-offices, tickets are
rinsed of gravel rash
and smirking contours

An excerpt as follows:

> *...We do acknowledge*
> *that we've left you with*
> *skeleton staff, whenever the*
> *grown-ups are convalescing*

VI.

Commissioned sandcastles
now exact an entrance fee;
Pierced beach-balls
and traded mermaids

the punters go for miles—
kicked
and screaming

woman never wins,
but she learns well
how to drive the pilot crazy

financial padding
does not provide long warranty
We perform on a
verbal command;
Indeed, the 'ol
neighbouring carnival of dogs
ought to bust up
the roaming circus of

perturbed rubber balloons

rabid wetsuits
smelling of stolen fish: (quiet...
the women are home now)
supper is boiling; seaweed
brewing
in heifer's strangling vapour

VII.

bury us in packages:

Ladies, drained
of chocolate grins, ask that you
send refuse overseas
via lifeboats
and floated companies,
  ... are we all worthy
of releasing itinerant
messages in seafaring bottles?

No embellishments here:
'Tis the simpleton who
rejects the aftertaste of
society's cultured pearl

(and rightly so)

The international recipe
has touted selfishness
as a worldwide delicacy (resembling
    the blubbering of
fatuous tongues)
The national recipe insists that
purchasing power
is a segmentary affair,
endorsed by half-a-dozen appetites

(two tenets affectively upheld):
Reiterate and

Conclude—shoving
miscellany into
the melting-pot ~ ~ ~

~ ~
~ ~ ~ ~ ~
~ ~ ~ ~ ~
~ ~ ~ ~   ~ ~ ~ ~ ~

VIII.

¼
- -
½
- -
Perchance you may
notice that
our oldest executive
has gained a strong reputation
 for mispricing; XXX
The unrectified trends of expenditure
have succeeded after his decades

needless to say he's unravelling...
As he unwittingly sports more
bandages, intangible costs
are steadily rising;
Consequently, the kids are
prone to tiptoeing 'round him

Before too long, they'll be
resounding without basis,
and he'll be stipulating that I wipe
his thorny mouth and rosy cheeks

black tie isn't rainproof
and I'm waiting
for deaf admission

)) (a huge impediment)

as the well-heeled populace
wrings out a regal return,
the mainstream tries to comprehend
a hardnosed fact—
toting up a treasury of tears
swelling in paramount delusion

← first-hand attention is compulsory
in this pristine food chain

IX.

Liquid assets are lured
towards ownership and tricked
into blindest possession;
visages renowned for
mopping up
tenuous pledges
left soaking in whitewash

Gentlemen, we drink twice to
your celebrations,
wheresoever you've been milking
partial standard

smashing lass—
 let her hold up her mirror
for the next seven years

good luck, virtue is crumbling

Even the sky could
see it recurring...
you failed me son,
Or is that your
grandfather orating to us both?

kind saviour
is degenerating, imploding in
  his | idle | sanity |
he is regulating the
    retention of anger \♀/

Mark my holy|*f*|words

frocks
  bless the warming of feet
and squires refresh
the mighty assessment
of liability;
outside a saturated perimeter,
watery stature
pours onto subjective terrain

soiled expectation kisses
importance as a
squalid afterthought;
dignified opinion
is traipsing haphazardly
  and presentiment is weighing

(shining Night—was adroitly
mounting shadows)

stalemate: Come along boys,
where did you forget to be
placid men—
walking mother's flaccid territory?

Dressing the Skeleton

The roses are gruffly
articulating,
 svelte memoirs
blowing dour smoke rings

Gesturing from their
garden beds, they query
the groundsman as to
why he posits them
in discomfited parade

He smiles upon their
fretting aspect,
intrusively
patting down dirt
around their naked ankles;
Clarification is
neither in his field of duty
 nor florescent endeavour,
  and so he is neatly
disembroiled of charges

Subdued amidst a stack
of flowerpots (exhausted
 by
merrymaking events)
resides the Lady Florence—
She is waiting for night space,
killing time until twilight,
 and pressing debilitated buttons
of visitors;
jet-lagged victims
     grazing the stark assertion
next to headstones:

None here ◇ ◇ ◇
open socio-economic doors
to estranged souls,
or spiced tempers–
Engineered suicide notes
will meet with
standard death in Las Vegas

Hydrating under his gazebo
of introspect,
one sunless gent
is
holding his breath
 underwater,
marvelling at the
hunting-ground of
dewless bathers leaving paw prints

Browsing fashionistas
encircle the garden,
noting home-grown fossils
swigging cocktails
and snoring through blindfold,
 as
bleary-eyed poets
turn soberly in their graves

Inaudibly,
the Lady Florence is
crocheting flowers
to pin onto fresh shirts and jerseys;
elevated offenders
are tweaked in passing,
 kissed frugally
by dwindling breezes;
She is lighting cigars,
obliging memories and long thoughts,
 while their
judgements are kicking stones

As evening falls into oblivion,
she is erasing now the people

       [successively,]
  all those
tiring,
    and nondescript
        human faces.

Part 3: The Reconstitution of Desire

Milk and Honey

a preamble:

*you call this white
man's suburb, but folks
are intruding from
every continent—
assorted troupes
enter in thru a
conspicuous portal;*

*in that rendered space
is a subtle place
 of
examination:*

*an amortised spectrum
 revising the
colour of money ~//*

~

now the compilation:

*revolving premises
it's the same old western
story; oriental blasphemy
> it seems as if glue
were bonding them
to ascribed tolerance*

*the concept of courtesy
is disgustingly bloated,
 such
brute community forming
spic 'n' span conventions*

[you're miffed]
'even as we strip the shirt
from your back,
don't be surprised—
it is not unusual to appear
less endowed, we are
harvesting your sensibility'
[one posy, two posies,
three posies,
four...]

tune in:
while cast members will
revel in the onslaught,
ordinary viewers
may not be aware of
tiered interpretations when
substituting wedding cakes
for one of our
famed postulations

[upon receiving wares,
we will despatch an apology]

~

the banter of energy
infiltrates life
give up portentous demands
of your index finger
and stop pointing,

head is partitioning
quantity into feasible slices
[and edible versions]

religion
is stirring rainclouds

above houses,
aristocrats wringing
  pretensions
from low mortality rates

essence
is extracting grapes
from perfectly healthy
persons with
emotional burdens
in need of renovation

binoculars are
narrowing the scope of
silence
(linear landscapes
squashed like accordions)
we don't buy back
unnatural predictions;
mental uterus
shares styles of inception,
and could you nicely trim
the
abdominal beef from
my cabbage leaves???
grinding connoisseurs
taking whiff of their
armpits
            [imputed
sexuality ^ ^ ^ ^ spicing up the
  ragbag of relations]

top-notch chef
has scuffed shoes, his galoshes
make for
sturdy place in the
kitchen (behind cow's rump),
horse has returned to the stables
after his wild trot;

*they are catering for
three navigators, all of whom
are wearing blinkers*

*and detonators
[mismatched firearms]*

*(and) who will each
by rights,
embody the
fourth squad*

(if staying alive…)

~

*$
suppose we sell @ cost price
?
improvising with a spoon
(patron fist requesting fork)
and kindly
keep that nasty knife
to one side of the table*

*the process
of curing solemnity
 locates gaping minutes of
adversity;
egg-timer
is set to military prompt
and booby-trapped schedule*

*a vast outlook searches for
for dandy welcomes—in place
of homecoming, we discover
myopic natives*

*grinning
maliciously
  (as far as the eye can't see)*

*yellow kite strings
snapping from unconscious
string-pulling*

*(teaching instructors spanked
black and blue)*

*the
copy cat had to
start
from his master's hand
  somebody had to guide him
out of the milk pool
wise lapping at the
shoreline, as the
tide peaceably offers herself*

*she was
 converting melancholy by furtive
exertion*

mesmeric

~

*salubrious footsteps
manoeuvre towards a sand dune;
the headland is dented with
posing shrubs and dumped
importation, confiscated
from unsanitary quarantines
(crying echo
of a drowned china doll)
tourists with despoiled fingers*

snatching evergreen stem
from passing trees
in accord with perfidious terms
and dicey conditions;
surely they know that happiness comes
at the expense of another's misfortune?

(sorry, won't elucidate—)

wilting concentration
waits for the comet to return,
but he
is resting in stationary journey
to gather sanctum
and so unanswered questions
remain in
lethargic diagnosis,
brevity coughing in its own
turmoil
(scanning the relics of aptitude)

turn on
turn off

~

some anecdotes: " "

an englishman is counting
the lips on his fingertips,
exotic ladies kissing his
knees:
should they stand up to full
height, he will be offended
by their infatuation

(hence he is effecting threat)

intelligent men patrol
an abeyant platform: who will
keep printing headlines,
when the news has nothing
more to say?
quote:
i collect beautiful people,
material skins inclusive of
recycled envy and catwalk fur

humans and icons
all (evidently) reconstituted

one
* adding*
one
makes two fixed lives
[plus scenarios carved in equal half]

man and angel
swapped racing vehicles,
tip trucks seen
carrying boulders to heaven
* (wrong way, go back)*
traffic giants orbiting
around suburban utopia

(today is) mayday

scrap metal pays in full
the photographer's bills, whilst
father figure slots babe in a
peripatetic stroller - - - - make way
* for its*
teeny tiny progress

(what, no one's steering?)

*chairlift is wrenching the
snow bunnies up by their ears
(o, what cute and muffled screams!)*

*superficiality
is caked on;
monday to friday left welts
and contusions
nineteen of them are made out
to look like love bites
[behold our grafted emotions]
>> loose zippers of the mother
forgave cut-price haberdashery
 'cause she, too, had rubescent
buttons popping from the rear*

*(so why was yin
  contesting yang ? ((
                    ((
               ((
            ((
don't know...)*

~

*alas!
original phobia has endured
a nagging overdose
and now denial is escalating
heroine may collapse at
any
moment,
then no one will be truly amused—
except maybe god,
who was tracking her disorderly arm
since elementary school*

smack:)

*supreme clownface; he's wearing
her makeup—she's
converging with irreverent pride
he thinks:
hasn't she forgiven me yet?
it's been so long that i laughed
heartily, or extended a wide yawn*

[rehearsed comfort]

*unceremoniously, her garter
has wrapped around his ankles,
inconveniencing the
alchemy
of benighted relatives*

*tête-à-tête: note too, over there,
that emphatic chap? well, of course
he took the impinging bait
[with her animus
superbly
delineating the
role of familial upset]*

but who's insinuating?

~

my own emergency

huh?

*i [got
caught in a maelstrom:]]*

doors, walls, windows

*have blocked the
entrance; i can't write my way
out of this maze
no theoretical winner:
only collective sperm
and an impatient lover*

*no lamplight
    firelight
        torchlight*

no sunburst either...

*and
stimulus is over the moon*

*ahh, would you excuse me at once
my mentor is waiting,
his unremitting patience
is holding my patriotism
[spy-hole to my guilty innocence]*

*a lifesaver!! he's extending out
the blanket of recuperated thoughts
 fittingly then,
let us remember together :::::
the roadway is sewn with
memorabilia;
this voyage of intrigue
gave no straight clues
to decipher
... and my logarithms
are less elastic than
they used to be
(microeconomy is expandable)
had you not shown me
cotton,
i would not have faltered*

*in my
synthetic upbringing*

*the physicist
and the eccentric—
i'm not sure who is whom,
since both are lately squabbling*

*damn this irritated anatomy
and its montage of
 irritable symptoms;
the medicine ball
sits
in my spring-cleaned corner,
ready for the next health blitz*

~

incidentally,

*old friends bet on a jockey
 and he lost;
they forgot which drunken
game they were playing,*
*- - - - - - losing streaks pursuing
a trail of clenched victory
    (... along with the tell-tale signs
of a scratched horse)*

*three used wishes
!   !   !*

*backs newly slumped until
depression kicks in;
jockey realizes he has just
turned into the punter //
// now he knows he is betting
on his own life*

```
        //
          //
            //
            //
              //
                //
//
  //
    //
          -----//--------//-- -- --
//
---// he is reprehensibly faced
   --- / --- with past competitors
```

(the splendour of triumph
  digests
rapidly:)
thus an unhinged man
fast loses the title of breadwinner;
simultaneously,
he is trading in his forearm
for an apron—
fluid kilojoules injected
more bulging numbers;
so now the worldly slant
has turned to woman
   [...observe how she rampantly
climbs that career ladder,

pantyhose need only slip once
that she's barefoot again]

~

!! thrilled !!

you're googling the A-side:

jack-o'-lantern
encounters
will-o'-the-wisp

i'm googling the B-side:
  fairy seeks flatmate

we're an eyeballing duo

ha, ha, ha, large word laughs
(we elate in jostling verbs)
read the fine print
on all coupons
you accepted
as a gift—

though wait!

as one of a kind,
you are cordially invited
to a barbecue:
they are registering names
from newest property estates

[inside the global box]
  you'll be supplied
with lunch napkins &
  plentiful forewarning—
these guests are bloodthirsty

[mandatory instructions]
customers to exit
at the licensee's request >
and so you must comply

manipulative insects
spotted in uniform: courtyard dining
  [dying from hallucination]
waitress to

abandon the melon for protein

~

one-one thousand,
two-one thousand...

first attend to the blemished crowd,
then peer in the social portfolio:
see
 if you see a fish
swimming in circles

swallowed birthstones
  (oppressed gestation)
life supporters
act as a healing apparatus
  [rocking passions]
humane corporations
soon-to-be the urban alternative

truth is purring...

we tell parts of our story,
so the whole is never heard
sustainable regrets
renewable nostalgia/
 mutual
scrapbook of memories

(a minefield of
pecking gossipers
  has the hubbub moving interstate)

~

an addendum:

can you send off the facsimile?
it's now or never

(no, it was not on the agenda)

confined group has virgin interest
in ethical investments;
man is financially stoking
his retirement,
woman is strategically
considering his meltdown
within
 the
hierarchy of apish ignorance

appallingly, some stride around
with turtle eggs, acquired
from sick animals
with retarded impulses;
harmonies condensing to chorus
piece-by-slaughtered-piece;
god is moderating relief
man is belching gluttony
unanimous voters say 'yes',
but will they ever agree on tactic?

we are
weighing bad dreams
by the tonne: transient values
of modern infrastructure
mr. romance brought along
his briefcase,
mr. analyst tripped over
his folding notebook

[contemporary devices and
unfashionable jargon]

*a run-down of heroes
may be listed by sumptuous nickname
(in block capitals please)*

*illicit emails unopened
deserted veterans
require a long-winded
exposition of changes;
what did they neatly salvage
by
removing
the vendor*

from his prospecting endeavours?

*survival of the fattest:
pecuniary indigestion
got buttered up marginally
for profit*

*disqualifying
toy chest: illustrators
are resigning
and resorting
to soapy imitations*

*[put all your dirty paintbrushes
in the one basket of eggs]*

*organic ego has no immunity
to
refrigeration this side of
the hemisphere (even where they
admired the handiwork of cortex)*

*'twas a greedy crown of thorns
ate god's entire stomach.*

Eclipse

[: vowel movements]
become
the feat to relinquish

Her own way
of unwinding: she's
so pent up that His
sporadic blessings
only add to bedlam
    : (excepting
an   interim of
    maenads)
They will
carry her out
wiping sap from gums
and twining leaves

he has monopoly
on
espresso equilibrium
in this smoke-filled oasis

spurned celebrity;
  an alliance of Healer
will decide
to sacrifice or to save;
ten minutes
realized ten years late
Rain-cloud soft as
bricks
could not wake them up

  (resuscitated defeat)

Heavenly rift:
  the conflict of inner winds

[disjointed] lashes

Adding squares
in quilted linen,
and rows of cottonseed
amidst
bedridden triangles

Surfeit—was typically
 uniting families
 with infantile personas

 boycotted addiction
 is without resolution
    Even when
 reducing to its lowest
 common denominator

 We are
 oscillating between
 changes,
 indulging in bias
 and podgy intentions;
  Silent movies
 would be aligning
 the vertebrae
 of painted lady
 and public misfit—unless
 the civilised trapeze act
has a fracture zone/
  /or
 colliding decibels

 [No Admittance]:
     Rutted flesh of killjoy
 was not extrapolated
 by way of panting casualties

 Warriors

keeping guard,
monitoring anti-climax
whilst atman
is brooding in his parlour,
seeking a reversible oracle

stone-ground prayer
will not respond to a
 fraught inquiry;
immobilise the pigtails
    during pantomimes,

(without pause) serve up
next metal replica.

Parting Wave

i)

What are you doing to earn
the price of a surf,
mister earth?
resentment stinks, then sinks
and I know because
I'm a larger
body of water than you

(yes ma'am)...The welcome mat
of rebuke
has gloating threshold
by its peppered invitation

your actions scored well today
eight and a half points
minus the sunshine;
so who really won?
Individuality
is a controversial area

move over,
sit down next to your trophy,
and contemplate your trivial
commotion
when gait has been
smothered under aqueous furore

Utter not a word
while daughter is chasing inflation
she may be flicking channels
by remote cognition,
your undisclosed interests
have somewhat
aroused her inborn suspicion

magnetic attraction is built
by industry experience (&
the Serious or circumspect)—
in hindsight, you will
appreciate these recommendations
 (then again...youth is rarely prudent,
even in the face of a reciprocal pulley)

ii)

succumb to the tidings
mister earth,
and do not grieve
the misconception of emotion

for until now,
you have made indiscriminate
selections
There is [sprightly] feeling
that soon it will be raining canines
and heaven's match will be
licking the flames ever after

Yowling axis shall compress
to ice-smooth temperament
each time that nanna
is caressing wet whiskers

she snaps a tremulous Polaroid:
 Agog
is the bazaar of entrepreneurs

(acuity
To be continued...) ∞

iii)

enigmatically, my birth cord
has twirled around your leg;

naturally,
you are not impressed—
you are cavorting in the
magnitude of virtuosity
and so can't suspect why (> judging
 by the
lack of amiable ventilation)

winning pleats are hoisted up
by mezzanine groundswell,
provocative jargon
is squeezing
out of maillots—
 it's the underlying
malaise of queenhood

eyes are stuck
 in
congealed perception,
The ministers of movability
have wax on their eyelashes

Childless uncles
ensuring that gorillas
reverse into their kennels,
then wait for owners
to pull the trigger
 on
phantom apathy

pre-mixed storytellers
selling us
their pocket-money,
The carbonated surrealist
is imbuing snobbery
with allied publicist,
whilst they meet
in between
modular furnishings

fabled argument is
petering out...
    (goodbye, mister earth)
... ...

iv)

The travelogue wraps up
in summary:

bandaged landforms and
the debris of busy-bodies,
blackest
Ants strutting undercover
of smouldering paperbacks

Whirlpool of recourse
 has been scattering on the
surface,
    gawking boats
diluting in the background
[alongside
blushing boys
and their medallions]

while
mesdames were rectifying merit.

Private Address

I.

Eliminate the barriers
to entry >< >< ><

Dearest Lieutenant:
Why don't we all
work for the army?

Then we could
genuinely admit
we adore being enlisted
to kill someone else's dream,
and let a haughty forecaster
spend his pay-packet on
yet another fulsome pleasure

[: renew the grit on pizza slabs]
make certain her etiquette
is not shy,
and that she gets
toughest helping with the lot

Truth is:
modest ladies look as if
they're preponderating,
engaged—never to be married

Should we courteously
slam down another cold coin?
 (this race, seems to be
imposing a requisite token)

dance, you drizzly raindrops
teetotalling is hardly
your illustrious pastime;

\- - >   - - >   [reload some Я & Я]   - - >

come --u- n-D--o-N- e

then reassemble at № 9;

(*I expect that*)   >> One great day
   you'll bluntly remember
the tweed suit,

 and flashing torso

Or was it grey? like
day trading
    sudden midnight...
Thank you for ambushed attending
but we are indifferent
to applause, because failure is
common in compassion's industry

however, we do sympathise with
propaganda—as our simple duchess
and nimble ally;
Money is without moral; swallow it,
and see how well
you can stomach the pulp of
an oozing tree...then witness
its shareholders
partake in a megalithic bath

[hey! my bungalow is right fit,
 but not
 a perfect match]

Injurious players
and smug exchange
provoked an inauspicious gamble
with today's
sundial

high – low

Find yourself
laughing into the world again
when you enter the realm
of puppies,
Ignoring their immaculate reflection
in the dry biscuit bowl

Negated outlays
    &
       newborn disbursement;
brash concerns dropped into the void
(for incineration purposes only):
Where they didn't quite bond
with interiors, they were
left like half-decorated collages

    [: look out for cinema-goers
tinged with homemade vanity]

Who's believing
your story, miss Apocalypse?

II.

Recapitulate:
a decapitated priest
is speechless,
branch manager
is dragging his corporate profile

(and corporeal effluence has
switched mouthpieces)

Though twenty-eight days
will channel into purest dimension,
the latter bloke may not be
in alkaline agreement—

(his shorthand believes twenty-one)

blah blah,

    and blah

The Issue of Serenity is customarily
scrambled, so you see why cynicism
is my trademark;
noxious breath of daily updates has
let the windmill run on vulgar numbers

Hold steady, and your
muse will follow you...
never mind
that ruthless conglomerates could
bank upon the speculative notion

nil dividend is a rest point
while leaning
over the edge of a translucent cliff

the supernatural explains reality
as
a hyphenated Stopwatch:
(superlatives ushered in my senses)
Rapturous punch-line: News reads:

"Britney Doll Replaces Barbie
as New Millennium Tragedy"

philosophy is covertly bundled up
in teenage preconceptions;
narrow-minded commodities
are struggling for power, small men
nestled among personal ads
and grimy prams
being taken for their stroll
 by

flitting nannies
with exaggerated composure

Of each,
 they will undermine her gaiety,
knowing she is tied into context
by burning wrists
and maternal rancour / Lush behaviour
saves for the circular saw

Tattered sarcasm:
there's an enormous hole in that woman

she has cross-legged merriment,
officers a bit slow in soothing a furrowed
brow
Exfoliated instincts—
where enlightenment mourned
to reach the crown

 embalmed devotion,
then we spilled beatitude on barest skin

vacant breast,
he's homesick for starched habitat.

About the Author

Dianne Cikusa was born in Sydney, Australia. Her writing has appeared in a number of online journals, poetry zines, anthologies, print magazines and as digital media.

In 1994, Dianne graduated with a Bachelor of Commerce from the University of Wollongong and later completed there a Graduate Diploma in Arts (Modern Languages) in 2010. In 2014, she further obtained a Diploma of Language Studies from the University of Sydney, majoring in French.

Hope and Substance is an amalgamation of two earlier written chapbooks of poetry, originally prepared under different titles.

Acknowledgements

I wish to thank Dr David Reiter and Kimberley Macintyre for their assessment and review of this collection throughout various stages of its development, as well as their valuable suggestions for its improvement.

My appreciation also extends to the staff at Mosher's Business Support for their technical expertise and assistance regarding the final production and distribution of this work. I am equally grateful to all those who mentored and encouraged me towards the fruition of this writing project over the many years in which it took shape and eventually found its creative voice.

www.ingramcontent.com/pod-product-compliance
Lightning Source LLC
Chambersburg PA
CBHW070433010526
44118CB00014B/2026